★ ★ ★

Abraham Lincoln

Abraham Lincoln

Steven Otfinoski

AMERICA'S

16TH

PRESIDENT

Children's Press®
A Division of Scholastic Inc.
New York / Toronto / London / Auckland / Sydney
Mexico City / New Delhi / Hong Kong
Danbury, Connecticut

Library of Congress Cataloging-in-Publication Data

Otfinoski, Steven.
    Abraham Lincoln / by Steven Otfinoski.
     p. cm. — (Encyclopedia of presidents. Second series)
    Summary: A biography of the sixteenth President of the United States.
Includes bibliographical references and index.
 ISBN 0-516-22887-0
   1. Lincoln, Abraham, 1809–1865—Juvenile literature. 2. Presidents—United
States—Biography—Juvenile literature. [1. Lincoln, Abraham, 1809–1865. 2.
Presidents.] I. Title. II. Series.
E457.905.O85 2003
973.7'092—dc22   2003018666

Contents

An Unlikely Leader

On April 14, 1865, President Abraham Lincoln and his wife Mary went to Ford's Theatre in Washington, D.C., to see a light comedy. It was one of the happiest days of Abraham Lincoln's presidency. He had begun his new term less than six weeks earlier. The terrible Civil War was coming to an end. Victorious northern forces had captured Richmond, the capital of the rebellious southern states. On April 9, General Robert E. Lee had surrendered his Army of Northern Virginia to northern general Ulysses S. Grant. Throughout the North, people were celebrating the end of the bloody war.

Midway through the third act, a shot rang out in the president's box at Ford's Theatre. President Lincoln slumped forward. His attacker jumped down onto the stage, shouted something to the audience, and hobbled off the stage and out the back door. Abraham

Lincoln, shot in the back of the head, never regained consciousness. He died the next morning.

Suddenly, celebrations turned into mourning. This unlikely president, whose election had been one cause of the Civil War, was dead. He had led the Union (the northern states) to victory over the Confederacy (the southern states) after four years of bloody civil war. In the weeks to come, millions would line up along the railroad tracks as his body was carried from Washington to his home in Springfield, Illinois. Yet many in the Confederacy refused to mourn the Union president who helped defeat their cause.

Who was this unlikely president? At a time when the average man stood 5 feet 4 inches tall (1.63 meters), Lincoln was 6-foot-4 (1.93 m), with long arms and legs. Many who saw him in person described him as ugly, calling him a "scarecrow" and a "gorilla." His speaking voice was high pitched. Even so, many who met him were captured by his warmth, his sense of humor, and his modesty. His enemies in the South considered him a tyrant or a dictator; his enemies in the North thought him a poor president, too indecisive and slow to act. Yet through his speeches and actions, he became a symbol of the Union's determination to end the slavery of African Americans and to create a new and unified nation.

Today, historians agree that Lincoln was one of our most important presidents. His actions and words helped change the course of the nation's history.

There are still many mysteries about the man and his achievements, however. Historians still are asking, Who was Abraham Lincoln?

Frontier Childhood ─────────────────────

Abraham Lincoln was born on February 12, 1809, on a farm near Hodgenville, in Hardin County, Kentucky. His father, Thomas Lincoln, was a farmer who supplemented his income doing carpentry work. Thomas had been born in Virginia and moved to Kentucky (then still part of Virginia) with his family as a child. When Thomas was eight years old, he was working in the fields with his father and two brothers when Indians attacked. His father was killed, and young Thomas was nearly captured.

As a young man, Thomas worked as a laborer and a carpenter to earn money for a farm of his own. In 1806, he married Nancy Hanks. Their first child, Sarah, was born the next year. In February 1809, Nancy Lincoln gave birth to a son in a cabin on the farm near Hodgenville. He was named Abraham after his grandfather.

Before Abraham was two years old, his family moved to another Kentucky farm. Then in 1816, when he was seven, they moved across the Ohio River to Indiana (which became a state that year). One of Thomas Lincoln's reasons for moving was that Indiana law prohibited slavery. Kentucky was a slave state, and

This log cabin is a replica of the one Abraham Lincoln lived in as a small boy on Knob Creek Farm in Kentucky. It was about 16 by 18 feet (4.8 by 5.4 m), had a single room, and a dirt floor.

the better land there was being bought up by plantation owners who used slaves to cultivate their crops. Thomas disapproved of slavery, and he felt he had a better chance to succeed in a region where he did not have to compete against slave labor. Young Abraham first learned about the issue of slavery from his father.

A New Mother

The Lincolns settled in a forested region on Little Pigeon Creek in southwestern Indiana. The first year was difficult. Neighbors helped the family build a new log cabin, but clearing the f̶ ... n even bigger job. Abraham was

... He learned to use an axe and helped his

... grew, he helped his father plant, care for, and harvest

Only a year after the Lincolns arrived in Indiana, tragedy struck. Nancy r̶ ... suddenly of "milk sickness," caused by milk from cows that had grazed on the poisonous snakeroot plant. Thomas made his wife's coffin himself buried her on a nearby hill. Her death was a hard blow for Thomas and his children.

Thomas soon realized he couldn't manage the farm and raise his two children alone. He returned to Kentucky in search of a wife. There he met Sarah Bush Johnston, a woman he had known before he married Nancy Hanks. Sarah was now a widow with three children. Thomas and Sarah were married in December 1819, and Thomas brought Sarah and her three children back to Indiana.

Sarah found the Lincolns' Indiana farm "wild, and desolate." The Lincoln household was in disarray and the Lincoln children were in need of attention and love. Sarah soon gained their confidence, treating them with as much affection as her own children. Although barely able to read and write herself, she encouraged Abe's reading and his desire to make something of himself.

Abraham had little time for school. His father needed the help of all the children to work on the farm. Besides, most schools at the time cost money to attend, and money was scarce. In total, Abe went to school for less than a year. "There was absolutely nothing to excite ambition for education," he wrote years later in a short presidential campaign biography. "I could read, write, and cipher [do simple arithmetic] . . . but that was all. I have not been to school since."

Still, Lincoln seemed fascinated by books and loved to read. The only book his family owned was a family Bible. As he grew older, he met neighbors who had other books, and he would walk miles to borrow them. Among his favorites were *Robinson Crusoe*, *Aesop's Fables*, and a life of George Washington.

Abraham's parents became members of the Pigeon Creek Baptist Church when Abe was 14, but he himself was never baptized. In his later life, he became a deeply religious person, but he never formally joined a Christian church. This may be partly due to the dissension he saw as a child within the Pigeon Creek church. As a young man, he did enjoy imitating the speech and mannerisms of local preachers and politicians to entertain his friends and neighbors.

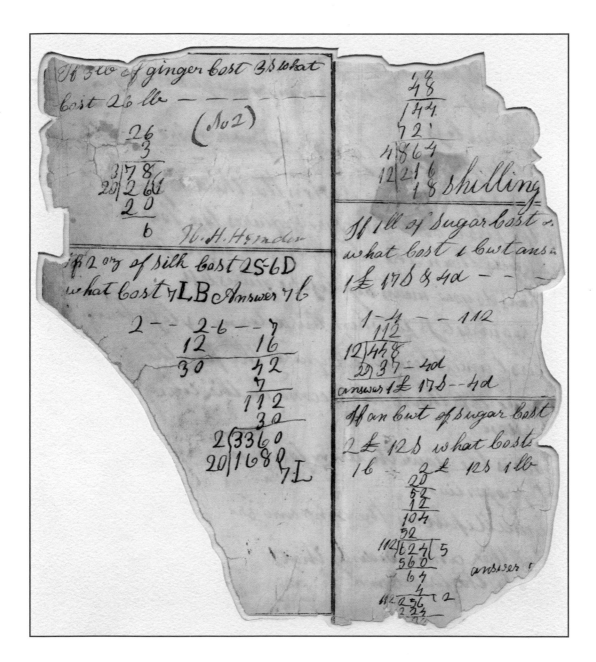

A scrap of the notebook in which young Abraham Lincoln practiced his arithmetic.

From Youth to Manhood ——————

In 1828 the 19-year-old Lincoln left home for the first time. He traveled with the son of a local merchant on a flatboat down the Ohio River to the Mississippi, then down the Mississippi to Louisiana, delivering farm goods to sell in New Orleans. The two young men had many adventures and were amazed at New Orleans, a much larger city than they had ever seen before.

On his two trips to New Orleans, Lincoln helped steer a flatboat like this one.

After he returned to Indiana, Abraham found it more and more difficult to get along with his father, who could not understand his wanting to better himself. Abraham continued to do much of the work on the farm, but he also took odd jobs in nearby towns and spent time with young men his own age.

In 1830 Thomas Lincoln again felt the urge to move west. He moved to a farm on the north bank of the Sangamon River near Decatur, Illinois, where the farmland was rich. Lincoln stayed with his parents long enough to help plant their first crop, but his disagreements with his father grew worse. Abraham had decided he did not want to be a farmer like his father.

In 1831, Denton Offutt, a local businessman, hired Lincoln and his cousin John Hanks to build a flatboat and take it down the Mississippi to New Orleans with a load of goods for sale. Now 22 years old, Abraham was legally an adult. He left home for good to make his own way in the world.

Chapter 2

Store Clerk and Soldier ——————

After returning from New Orleans, Lincoln settled in the village of New Salem, Illinois, on the Sangamon River, about 40 miles (64 kilometers) west of his father's farm. Businessman Denton Offutt owned a general store there and offered him a job as a clerk. The townspeople were amazed at Abraham's height and strength, and they were soon captivated by his gentle personality and wry humor. Lincoln liked the people of New Salem, too. Before long, he was looking for ways to help the town grow.

Seeing that Lincoln was a bright young man and that he had some experience on the river, leaders in New Salem urged him to run for the Illinois General Assembly, the lower house of the state legislature. There they hoped he could seek state funds to dredge and improve the Sangamon River to make it a major trade route. In March 1832, he announced that he would run.

Soon afterward, however, Denton Offutt's business ventures failed—including the store where Lincoln worked. Without regular work, Abraham found it necessary to make a living by taking odd jobs. When the governor of Illinois sent out a call for volunteers for the state militia to fight in the Black Hawk War in northern Illinois, Lincoln signed up for 30 days of service. The volunteer militiamen elected their own company officers. Lincoln's company thought so much of Lincoln that they elected him their captain. Years later, Lincoln said his election as captain "gave me more pleasure than any I have had since."

After his 30 days, Lincoln reenlisted for two more 30-day terms. In his brief service, Lincoln never saw an Indian or engaged in any military action. He wrote later about his service, "I fought a good many bloody struggles with the mosquitoes."

In the summer of 1832, Lincoln returned to New Salem, only weeks before the elections for the General Assembly. There were 13 candidates in the race, and the top four would be elected. Lincoln wasn't well known enough to have a real chance. He finished eighth, but he received nearly every vote cast in New Salem.

After his election defeat, he stayed in New Salem, looking for a job. In January 1833, he bought a general store with William F. Berry, an old militia friend. They borrowed money to pay for the store and its goods. Most people

The Black Hawk War

In 1831 the Sac and Fox Indians agreed to leave northern Illinois and settle on a reservation across the Mississippi River in Iowa. In the spring of 1832, however, a chief named Black Hawk led a group of about a thousand back into Illinois to reclaim their ancestral lands near present-day Rock Island.

Federal troops, supported by the Illinois militia, drove Black Hawk's band up the Rock River into Wisconsin. Hungry and exhausted, the Native Americans were trying to return to Iowa when U.S. troops caught up with them on the shore of the Mississippi at Bad Axe, Wisconsin. Many were shot down or drowned trying to cross the river. Black Hawk was captured a few weeks later. He agreed to return to Iowa and give up all claims to land in Illinois.

At the Battle of Bad Axe, the people of Chief Black Hawk are trying to reach the Mississippi River, while their fighting men (in the background) are slowing down the U.S. army troops.

☆★☆

shopped at other stores, however, and Lincoln's store failed in a few months. Soon afterward, Berry died. Lincoln promised that he would repay Berry's share of the debt as well as his own. He paid off every penny, but it took him 17 years.

These buildings are replicas of those in New Salem in Lincoln's day. Like Lincoln, nearly all the residents moved away over the years and the original town disappeared.

In May 1833, Lincoln was appointed postmaster of New Salem. The job didn't pay much, and there was no post office. Lincoln received the mail twice a week and handed it out at a local store. He delivered mail that no one picked up, sometimes carrying it in his hat. Before delivering newspapers, he read them. Lincoln also worked as deputy to the county surveyor. He knew nothing about surveying but soon mastered the subject by reading books about it. Surveying took him to many parts of the county, where he met the farmers and merchants in the surrounding area.

A Start in Politics

In 1834, Lincoln ran again for the General Assembly as a member of the new Whig party. This time he was elected to one of the county's seats. Now 25 years old, he borrowed $200 to buy a new suit and other necessary items to make a good appearance when he arrived in Vandalia, then the state capital.

In the General Assembly, Lincoln met John T. Stuart, a fellow legislator and a successful attorney in Springfield, a growing town 10 miles (16 km) from New Salem. Stuart soon convinced Lincoln that he should become a lawyer. Law students in those days studied with a practicing lawyer, and Stuart offered to serve as Lincoln's teacher. Several times, he walked the 20-mile (32-km) round-trip to Springfield to borrow books from Stuart's library to study in his spare time.

During this time, Lincoln began a friendship with Ann Rutledge, whose father owned the tavern where he roomed. When they met, Ann was already engaged to another man. As the months passed, however, a romance began to blossom, and Ann planned to break off her engagement. Then in the summer of 1835, Ann came down with a severe fever and died. Lincoln was devastated by her death. Historians do not know how serious the romance really was, but for the rest of his life, Lincoln found it difficult to discuss his relationship with Ann Rutledge.

In his first term in the General Assembly, Lincoln listened and learned. He was reelected in 1836 and became the leader of the Sangamon County delegation,

The old State House in Vandalia, Illinois, which was the state capital when Lincoln was elected to the state legislature.

which gained the nickname "the Long Nine" because the total height of the nine delegates was 54 feet (16.2 m)—an average of six feet (1.8 m) each. In his first effort as a political leader, Lincoln led a campaign to move the state capital from Vandalia, in the southern part of the state, to Springfield, the largest and most promising town in Sangamon County. After a long battle, Springfield was finally chosen to be the new capital in February 1837.

Lawyer Lincoln

In September 1836, Lincoln received his license to practice law. New Salem was too small to have much need for lawyers. Lincoln decided to move to Springfield. He arrived on a borrowed horse in April 1837 and became a junior partner in John Stuart's law practice. Four years later, Lincoln went to work with Stephen T.

Riding the Circuit

The life of a frontier lawyer in Lincoln's day was not easy. There was not enough law business in any central Illinois town to keep a lawyer busy. Instead, lawyers "rode the circuit" twice a year, traveling from town to town along with a circuit judge, trying cases of all kinds in one town after another. The circuit that Lincoln traveled usually covered eight or ten counties, and he was on the road for three months at a time.

Lawyers traveled by horseback or buggy along dirt roads that were frozen solid in winter and knee-deep in mud in the spring. They spent their nights in roadside inns and taverns where the food was often terrible and the conditions miserable. Yet Lincoln rarely complained about the conditions. He enjoyed the long, solitary rides across the prairie and the easy companionship of the lawyers in the taverns. He loved to tell old stories and collect new ones around the fireplace. He was still retelling many of these stories years later as president.

"In my opinion," one friend wrote, "Lincoln was happy, as happy as *he* could be, when on this circuit, and happy no other place."

☆ ☆ ☆

Logan, one of Springfield's most successful lawyers. Then in 1844, he opened his own practice, taking on young William Herndon as a junior partner. Lincoln was 35, and Herndon was 26. Herndon became a close friend of Lincoln's and one of his most devoted supporters. They would remain law partners until Lincoln's death. When Lincoln was away serving in political office, Herndon would carry on the practice by himself. In 1889, long after Lincoln's death, Herndon published a pioneering biography of his longtime partner and friend.

Lincoln practiced law from 1837 until he was elected president in 1861. During these years, he gradually built a reputation as one of the outstanding lawyers in Illinois. For most of his career, he was a generalist, performing nearly any legal task. He drew up wills, deeds, and other legal documents. He represented merchants and farmers in lawsuits over business disagreements. He defended people accused of criminal acts such as murder, robbery, and fraud. Like other lawyers, he sometimes defended people who were guilty, arguing in their defense to the best of his ability. On the circuit, he sometimes served temporarily as a judge when a regular judge was unavailable.

As Lincoln's practice grew, he engaged more partners and took more complicated cases. By the 1850s, he was representing railroads and other large corporations, but he continued to represent individuals and small businesses as well. In 1853, he took on one of the biggest cases of his career, a tax case for the

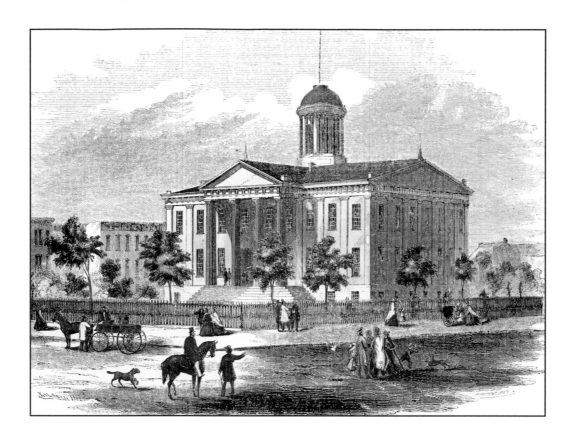

This State House was built in Springfield after it was named the new state capital. Lincoln often used the law library in the building. Today the State House has been replaced by a much larger state capitol building.

Illinois Central Railroad. He gained a court decision that saved the railroad millions of dollars and was paid $5,000.

During his years practicing law, Lincoln met nearly all the political and business leaders in Illinois. When he went into politics, his reputation as an honest and able lawyer was a big advantage. He was especially admired for his ability in the courtroom. One newspaper reported in 1850, "In his examination of witnesses, he displays a masterly ingenuity. . . . Bold, forcible and energetic, he forces conviction upon the mind, and, by his clearness and conciseness, stamps it there, not to be erased. . . . Such are some of the qualities that place Mr. Lincoln at the head of the profession in this state."

Courtship and Marriage ——————————————

In 1836, Lincoln and a woman named Mary Owens were informally engaged to be married. Both of them soon had second thoughts about their commitment. Lincoln wanted to break off the engagement, but he didn't want to hurt Mary's feelings. He tried many ways to get *her* to call it off. Finally, he wrote a letter almost begging her to break the engagement. He said she could break it by not answering. When she didn't answer, he was hurt. He later made a joke of the whole matter. He wrote to a friend, "I have now come to the conclusion never again to think of marrying, and for this reason: I can never be satisfied with anyone who would be blockhead enough to have me."

A few years later, in 1839, Lincoln met Mary Todd. She was the sister of Mrs. Elizabeth Edwards, whose husband, Ninian Edwards, was one of the most important men in Springfield. Mary was 20 years old, pretty and well dressed. She had an alert mind and a sharp tongue. She had grown up in a wealthy, cultured household in Louisville, Kentucky, and was much more polished than Abraham Lincoln. Yet for some reason, he found it easy to talk with her. During

Mary Todd Lincoln about 1846, a few years after she and Abraham were married.

1840, Abraham and Mary saw each other often. They agreed on politics, both favoring the Whig candidate for president that year, William Henry Harrison. Mary's family seemed pleased with the romance. Finally, in December, they were engaged to be married.

Again, Lincoln soon had second thoughts. How could he be sure Mary Todd was the right woman for him? How would he support her on his small lawyer's salary when she was used to wealth and comfort? He finally met with Mary and broke their engagement. She was shocked, but she soon agreed to call off their plans.

Lincoln fell into a deep depression. He took to his bed for a week and would not see visitors. His friends began to worry about him. Through the winter and spring, he remained depressed and unhappy. That summer, he made a visit to his old Springfield friend, Joshua Speed, who had moved to Kentucky and was engaged to be married himself. As the two discussed women and marriage, Lincoln seemed to relax. When he returned to Springfield, he had recovered from his depression.

Mary Todd was still living with her sister's family. At a party both Abraham and Mary attended, a mutual friend brought the two of them together and said, "Be friends again." They both seemed ready to make up. A few months later, on November 4, 1842, they were married at the home of Mary's sister and brother-in-law. Lincoln was 33 years old, and Mary Todd was 23.

The young couple rented rooms at the Globe Tavern, an inn. Their first child, Robert, was born there in 1843. Soon after his birth, the Lincolns rented a small house in Springfield. Then in 1844, they bought a modest home at the corner of Eighth and Jackson Streets. It had three rooms downstairs and two bedrooms upstairs. Here they would live and raise their family. They later enlarged and remodeled the house, but it remained their home until Lincoln was elected president.

On to Congress ──────────────────────

In need of money for his new family, Lincoln devoted much of his energy to his law practice. He had not forgotten politics, though. His Whig party was a minority in Illinois, so there was little chance he could win a statewide office. But in the Seventh Congressional District (much of central Illinois), Whigs were in the majority. This meant he might gain election to the U.S. House of Representatives.

Many Whig leaders in the district wanted to run for Congress, however. In 1843, the party nominated John Hardin. In 1844, the nomination went to Lincoln's friend in Springfield, Edward Baker. Finally, in 1846, it was Lincoln's turn. He won the nomination and was elected.

Abraham Lincoln in 1846, the year he was elected to the U.S. House of Representatives.

Even though he was elected in the fall of 1846, the first session of the new Congress did not begin until December 1847. Lincoln left the law office in the hands of his young partner. He rented out the Lincoln house. In October 1847, Lincoln, Mary, Robert (now four years old), and their younger son Eddie (not yet two) set off for Washington.

The Lincolns rented rooms in a Washington boardinghouse where many congressmen lived when Congress was in session. Since most congressmen left their wives at home, Mary had few friends and little to do. In the spring of 1848, Mary and the children left Washington and went to spend time with her family in Lexington. When Lincoln came back to Washington in late 1848, Mary and the boys stayed in Springfield.

When the Lincolns arrived in Washington, the city was celebrating victory in the U.S.-Mexican War. The United States, led by Democratic president James Polk, had declared war on Mexico the previous year. U.S. forces gained control of Mexico's northern provinces and captured the Mexican capital, Mexico City. In the treaty ending the war, Mexico gave up territory that included all or part of ten present-day states in the Southwest.

Like many Whigs, Lincoln had been against the war. He believed that President Polk had attacked Mexico on a flimsy excuse. He also opposed the main aim of the war—to gain huge Mexican territories for the United States.

Lincoln made a powerful speech in the House of Representatives against the war and its aims.

Many Whigs in Washington applauded Lincoln's speech, but his views were unpopular in his home district. The two Whig congressmen who represented the Seventh District before Lincoln had fought bravely in Mexico. In addition, many Americans were pleased that the United States would gain huge territories from Mexico. Lincoln's speech made it certain that the Whigs in his district would nominate a different candidate for Congress for the 1848 election.

Meanwhile, Lincoln began to campaign in several states for Zachary Taylor, one of the victorious generals in the U.S.-Mexican War, for the Whig nomination for president. Taylor was the most popular and

A campaign poster for Whig candidate Zachary Taylor in the 1848 presidential election. Lincoln favored Taylor and worked in the campaign. Taylor was elected.

admired man in America at the time, and Lincoln believed he could be elected on the Whig ticket.

When Zachary Taylor won the election, Lincoln hoped that his services to the Taylor campaign might help him gain appointment to a federal job. He hoped to become commissioner of the General Land Office, which involved selling government lands to new settlers in the West. The job went to someone else, however, and Lincoln returned to Springfield.

Forty years old, Lincoln was tired of the ups and downs of politics. It seemed that he was through with politics and would make his reputation as a lawyer. However, politics wasn't through with Abraham Lincoln.

Chapter 3

Law and Family

When Lincoln returned to Springfield in early 1849, his first concern was to revive his law practice, which had been too much for Herndon to handle alone. Lincoln later wrote that he worked harder at the law between 1849 and 1854 than at any time in his life.

Meanwhile, the Lincoln family suffered a painful loss. Late in 1849, young Eddie Lincoln, not quite four years old, came down with tuberculosis, a wasting disease for which there was then no cure. He died on February 1, 1850. Mary Lincoln grieved terribly. Lincoln said less, but he also suffered from the loss of his young son. By the summer, Mary Lincoln was expecting another child. In December she gave birth to William Wallace Lincoln, whom the family would call Willie. Then in 1853, the Lincolns welcomed their fourth and last child, Thomas, who gained the nickname Tad.

During these years, the law firm of Lincoln and Herndon was becoming one of the most important in Illinois. It was now beginning to represent railroads and other large corporations. Many of these cases were tried in Chicago, on the shores of Lake Michigan, which was rapidly becoming the most important city in the state. Law business from the railroads was making Lincoln a prosperous man. The railroads themselves were making his life easier. Since many towns on the circuit were connected to Springfield by rail, Lincoln could try cases during the week, then ride home by train to spend the weekend with his family.

Slavery

Abraham Lincoln might have finished his career as a leading lawyer in Illinois, but in 1854 he was drawn into the growing issue about the spread of slavery.

Slavery had been a subject of dispute ever since the early days of the United States. The Constitution of the United States, written in 1787, recognized slavery, but the word itself was never mentioned. The Constitution also provided that beginning in 1808 (20 years after it took effect), bringing new slaves into the country would become illegal. As the country grew, southerners began to worry that some future government might restrict or end slavery.

In 1819, slavery became a serious issue between North and South. When Missouri applied for statehood as a slave state, northerners were reluctant to agree. Henry Clay of Kentucky proposed that Missouri be admitted as a slave state together with Maine, which wished to be admitted as a free state. This compromise would keep the number of free and slave states exactly even. In addition, the compromise drew a line through the unorganized territory west of Missouri. North of this line, slavery would not be permitted; south of the line, it would be allowed. Known as the Missouri Compromise, the measure passed in 1820. It settled issues about slavery in new states and territories for 30 years. During that time, Congress admitted new states in pairs, one slave and one free, to keep the number of slave and free states even.

The spread of slavery became an issue again in 1850. In the previous five years, the United States had added huge new territories in the West. It received full possession of the Oregon Territory from Great Britain in 1846, and the vast southwest territories from Mexico in 1848. Many northerners, including Abraham Lincoln, wanted to make certain that slavery would not spread to these new territories. The southern states, which were producing nearly two-thirds of the world's cotton, were more dependent on slave labor than ever before, and southerners were looking for territory where they could expand their slave economy.

Henry Clay, now an old man, designed another compromise. California, where gold had been discovered in 1848, had applied to become a new free state, but there was no slave state to add as a balance. Clay proposed that California be

Henry Clay was a founder of the Whig party and one of Lincoln's political heroes. He was the architect of the Missouri Compromise (1820) and of the Compromise of 1850. He was a major candidate for president three times, but was never elected.

admitted to the Union as a free state, breaking the balance in the Senate. At the same time, a new *Fugitive Slave Act* would commit the federal government to help capture and return slaves who ran away to the North. After bitter debate, Congress passed this Compromise of 1850. One of its strongest supporters was Democratic senator Stephen Douglas of Illinois. Both sides found the compromise difficult to swallow. Many northern states previously refused to help hunt down runaway slaves and wanted to continue to do so. However, most moderate politicians (including Abraham Lincoln) supported the compromise.

The Kansas-Nebraska Act

By 1854, attention shifted to the Nebraska Territory, a huge region that included most of the old Louisiana Purchase—from the present-day states of Kansas and Nebraska, stretching north and west to the Canadian border. Settlers had begun arriving, and it was clear that the territory would be divided into new states in coming years.

Stephen Douglas of Illinois was the author of the proposed Kansas-Nebraska Act. He suggested that the Nebraska Territory be divided in two, creating the Kansas Territory in the south, just west of Missouri (a slave state), and the Nebraska Territory in the north, beginning just west of Iowa (a free state) and stretching far to the northwest. Both territories were north of the line drawn by the old Missouri Compromise, which required that any new state formed from the territories

Democrat Stephen Douglas, powerful leader in Illinois and in the U.S. Senate. The Kansas-Nebraska Act, which he wrote and helped pass, brought Abraham Lincoln back into politics. The two men ran against each other for the Senate in 1858 and for president in 1860.

prohibit slavery. Douglas proposed, however, that the choice of allowing or prohibiting slavery in Kansas and Nebraska be left to the people who lived in the territories. They would decide the issue by a vote. He called this "*popular sovereignty.*"

The proposal caused a huge outcry in the North, especially among those most opposed to slavery. The act "repealed" the Missouri Compromise, and would allow any new state to be admitted with a proslavery constitution if its residents voted for it. Douglas believed that this new compromise was necessary to persuade the southern states to stay in the Union. If both Kansas and Nebraska were admitted as free states, southern states were threatening to *secede*, or leave the United States. Douglas skillfully guided the Kansas-Nebraska Act to passage in both the House and the Senate, and President Franklin Pierce signed it into law in May 1854.

The new act caused a political crisis. Abraham Lincoln's Whig party was so badly divided over the Kansas-Nebraska Act that it was never an effective party again. Northern Whigs, those against the Kansas-Nebraska Act, and others who opposed slavery, worked to organize a new party that could represent them on this crucial issue. It would become the Republican party, and Abraham Lincoln would soon be one of its leading members.

Lincoln and Douglas

Lincoln saw the Kansas-Nebraska Act as an important new political issue. He followed events carefully and began to study the history of slavery and the issues surrounding it. In the fall of 1854, Senator Douglas returned to Illinois to defend the Kansas-Nebraska Act and to campaign for Democratic candidates in the state. On October 3, he appeared in Springfield, speaking for several hours to a sympathetic crowd. Lincoln was in the audience. As the crowd was leaving, Lincoln and his friends let the crowd know that Lincoln himself would answer Douglas the following day. They invited Douglas to come to answer Lincoln's speech.

Lincoln's speech the next afternoon made him a new political star. It also began a competition with Stephen Douglas that would continue for the next six years. Lincoln spoke for three hours. For the first time, he expressed his deepest beliefs about slavery. He described the difference between Douglas and himself as about "whether a Negro *is not* or *is* a man." If African Americans *are* men (human beings), Lincoln said, then the words of the Declaration of Independence apply to them—they are "created equal" and have rights to "life, liberty, and the pursuit of happiness."

Douglas spoke for two hours in reply, but Lincoln's speech created a sensation. One supporter wrote that Lincoln should attack Douglas "until he runs him into his hole or makes him holler 'Enough!'" The organizers of the Republican party realized that Lincoln could be one of their most powerful champions.

In the next few weeks, Lincoln agreed to become the Whig candidate for the U.S. Senate, opposing Douglas's candidate, James Shields. U.S. senators were then elected by state legislatures. In the fall elections, the Democrats won a majority of seats in the legislature, which made it difficult for Lincoln to gain election. When the legislature met to choose the new senator, the winner needed 51 votes. Lincoln was the leader in the first ballot, but he had only 45 votes. Democrats split between Shields and Lyman Trumbull, a Democrat who was against the Kansas-Nebraska Act. Lincoln saw that he could not win, so he threw his support to Trumbull. On the tenth ballot, Trumbull was elected.

The election was a defeat for Lincoln, but it was an even greater defeat for Stephen Douglas. His candidate lost the election, and members of his own party rejected the Kansas-Nebraska Act.

Abraham Lincoln, Republican ───────

Lincoln returned to his law practice again in 1855. He also became active in the new Republican party, which was gradually becoming the second major party in the northern states. For the 1856 presidential election, the Republicans nominated John C. Frémont for president. Lincoln campaigned for Frémont, but it was clear that the new party did not have the national membership or the organization to win the election. The Democrats, who could count on nearly all the votes in the South and many in the North, elected former Pennsylvania senator James Buchanan president.

Closer to home, the Lincolns carried out a major renovation of their house in Springfield. By adding a full second floor, they nearly doubled the floor area of the house. The house was painted while Lincoln was away on business and he scarcely recognized it when he returned. With a twinkle in his eye, he asked a passing neighbor, "Stranger, do you know where Lincoln lives?" Pointing at his own house, he said, "He used to live here."

The Lincoln home in Springfield, Illinois, as it looked after it was enlarged in 1855. Today it is a Lincoln museum.

The Dred Scott Decision ————————————————

In March 1857, only days after James Buchanan took office as president, the U.S. Supreme Court announced its decision in the case of Dred Scott. Scott had been a slave in Missouri. His owner, a military doctor, had taken Scott to live in Illinois and later in the Wisconsin Territory. Then they returned to Missouri. After his master died, Dred Scott brought suit against the government to claim his freedom, claiming that the years he lived in states and territories where slavery was illegal made him free.

In the majority opinion, Chief Justice Roger Taney wrote that as a slave, Dred Scott was not a citizen of the United States and as a black man had "no rights that a white man is bound to recognize." The decision also suggested that the federal government had no power to restrict slavery in the territories and that the Missouri Compromise was unconstitutional.

Lincoln made no public comment about the ruling. As a lawyer, he had always respected the courts and believed that the government depended on obeying court rulings. Still, the Dred Scott case shook his faith in the courts. It pleased Southerners, but in the North it caused angry demonstrations and brought new recruits to the Republican party. The decision further widened the gap between North and South.

The Lincoln-Douglas Debates ————————

In 1858, Senator Douglas was up for reelection to the U.S. Senate. The Illinois Republican party announced in June that its nominee for the Senate was Abraham Lincoln. In his acceptance speech, Lincoln made his position on the slavery issue very clear. Using a familiar saying of Jesus from the Christian scriptures, he said,

> "A house divided against itself cannot stand." I believe this government cannot endure, permanently half *slave* and half *free*. I do not expect the Union to be *dissolved*—I do not expect the house to *fall*—but I *do* expect it will cease to be divided. It will become *all* one thing, or *all* the other.

Lincoln challenged Douglas to a series of debates. Douglas reluctantly agreed. The two agreed to appear seven times between August 21 and October 15 in towns throughout the state. It was agreed that the first speaker would speak for one hour, the second would speak for an hour and a half, and then the first speaker would have the closing half-hour to reply.

The Lincoln-Douglas debates created a sensation in Illinois and across the nation. As many as 10,000 people came to hear a debate in person. Newspapers sent special correspondents who could take down the speakers' words in shorthand for publication soon afterward. Transcripts and long articles about the debates appeared not only in Illinois, but in major newspapers across the country.

The two men presented a strong contrast on the platform. Douglas was only 5-feet 4-inches (1.63 m) tall, but he had broad shoulders, a large head, and a deep, powerful voice. He was known as "the Little Giant." He dressed in the highest fashion, and presented himself as a polished political leader. Lincoln, at 6-foot-4 (1.93 m), was painfully thin, and his clothes seemed to hang on him like a scarecrow's. His gestures were awkward, and his voice was high pitched.

The debates focused on one subject, the spread of slavery. Lincoln insisted that it was a moral issue. Douglas replied that it was a political issue. Using every debating trick, the two entertained and informed their listeners. When the debates were over, both sides claimed victory.

On election day, voters of Illinois elected the state legislators who would choose the next senator. Many may have voted based on the issues raised in the debates, but many others voted based on local issues and personalities. Douglas's Democrats held their control of the legislature by a narrow margin. When the legislators met in early 1859 to elect a senator, Douglas received 54 votes and Lincoln received 46.

Lincoln was depressed by his loss, but he also realized that he had won something, too. He wrote to a friend, "[The race] gave me a hearing on the great

The Lincoln-Douglas debate in Galesburg, Illinois, was held at Knox College there. Thousands came out to listen to the debate, which lasted three hours.

and durable question of the age, which I could have had in no other way." He was now recognized as a spokesman for the Republican party.

A Taste for the Presidency

Lincoln went back to his law practice in Springfield, but his mind was still on politics. He often traveled to speak to Republican audiences throughout the northern states. He also spent time guiding the shaky Republican party in Illinois. It had many supporters, but they often disagreed with each other.

By the end of 1859, newspapers in Illinois and elsewhere were suggesting that Lincoln be the Republican nominee for president. The Democrats were deeply divided. President James Buchanan was widely unpopular. He and Douglas were struggling for control of the Democratic party. In the North, Democrats were losing support because their stand on the spread of slavery was very unpopular.

In February 1860, Lincoln was invited to make a major address in New York City. He presented a long, thoughtful speech on the history of the slavery question. At first, the New York audience was surprised by his strange appearance and his high, squeaky voice. As the speech went on, however, Lincoln charmed and persuaded his listeners. At the end, he urged them to work fearlessly against the spread of slavery. "Let us have faith that right makes might," he concluded, "and in that faith, let us, to the end, dare to do our duty as we understand it."

Behind the scenes, Lincoln worked with his allies to persuade Republicans to hold their nominating convention in Chicago. It would be the first convention held so far west, would help attract westerners to the party, and might also help Lincoln gain the presidential nomination.

The two most influential members of the new party were Senator William H. Seward of New York and Salmon P. Chase, a former senator and governor

Abraham Lincoln in a photograph taken the day he made a major speech in New York City in February 1860. The speech helped him gain the Republican nomination for president.

from Ohio. Seward was a conservative, still seeking compromise with the southern states. Chase was more radical, deeply opposed to slavery. Seward was favored to win the nomination for president, but he had made many enemies in the party.

Lincoln was not as well known to the delegates, but he had one big advantage—fewer enemies. He hoped to be the second choice of delegates who began by supporting other candidates.

He decided not to go to the convention himself, staying home in Springfield and receiving reports from the Chicago convention by telegraph. To be nominated, a candidate needed 233 votes. On the first ballot, Seward led with 173 votes, and Lincoln was second with 102. The rest of the votes were divided

The Wigwam was a huge wooden building built in Chicago to host the Republican National Convention in 1860. Here Lincoln was nominated for president. A few years later, the building burned down.

among many other candidates. On the second ballot, Seward still led with 184 votes, but Lincoln had 181. On the third ballot, Lincoln took the lead with 231 votes, only two short of victory. Four Ohio delegates switched to Lincoln, giving him the nomination. Then all the remaining delegates shifted their votes, making his nomination *unanimous*.

While the Republicans stood united behind their candidate, the Democrats were deeply divided. Stephen Douglas was the presidential choice of the northern wing of the party, but the southern Democrats refused to support him. They felt he was not ardent enough in his support of slavery, and they walked out of the convention. Later, they nominated Kentuckian John C. Breckinridge for president. To further complicate the election, the Constitutional Union Party (made up of southern Whigs) nominated former Tennessee senator John Bell.

Lincoln was often shown as "The Rail-Splitter" during the 1860 campaign. The image suggested that he was familiar with hard work on the frontier. A rail splitter splits logs into rails that can be used to build fences.

The election in November was one of the strangest in the country's history. Lincoln and the Republicans were very strong in the northern states, but they had no support at all in the South. Lincoln received more popular votes than any other candidate, with nearly 1.9 million. Douglas received nearly 1.4 million. Altogether, however, Lincoln received only 40 percent of the total vote. Together, his three opponents received 60 percent of the vote. In the *electoral college*, where state electors officially elect a president, Lincoln won a comfortable majority. He received 180 votes. Breckinridge received 72, Bell 39, and Stephen Douglas only 12. The most ominous news was that in many southern states, not a single voter cast his vote for Lincoln.

Chapter 4

Inauguration

Abraham Lincoln was elected in November 1860 and would not take office until March 4, 1861. Yet the effects of his election were felt immediately. Throughout the South, state political leaders expressed their fear that Lincoln's Republican administration would attempt to end slavery. They urged their states to secede from the Union. South Carolina seceded on December 20. Mississippi, Florida, Alabama, Georgia, and Louisiana declared their independence in January. These six states met on February 9 to form the Confederate States of America.

As each state seceded, its representatives and senators resigned their seats in the U.S. Congress and went home. The newly independent states began taking over federal *arsenals* and military bases in their territory. President Buchanan refused to risk war by sending federal troops to protect federal property. By March 1861, Lincoln faced a national crisis no other president-elect had ever faced—the dissolution of the country he had been elected to govern.

In the meantime, Lincoln and his family rented out their Springfield home and made preparations to move to Washington. Lincoln traveled in a special train, stopping along the way to address supporters in the northern states. When the train reached Philadelphia, Lincoln was warned that there was a plot to assassinate him when the train stopped in Baltimore. Maryland was still a part of the Union, but it was a slave state and many of its residents supported the South. With no announcement, he transferred to another train, which rolled through Baltimore at 3 A.M. He arrived safely in Washington early on the morning of February 23.

Lincoln was sworn in as the 16th president on March 4, 1861. Even though six states had seceded, Virginia and North Carolina, two of the South's largest states, had not left the Union. In addition, the slave states of Maryland, Delaware, Tennessee, Kentucky, and Missouri were still loyal. In his inaugural address, Lincoln stressed the long-standing friendship between the states and assured the South that it was not his object to end slavery in their states. He also stressed the vital importance of preserving the Union. In his closing paragraph, he said, "We are not enemies, but friends. We must not be enemies. Though passion may have strained, it must not break our bonds of affection."

In the inaugural procession, Lincoln is riding with outgoing president James Buchanan. This sketch was made for a magazine by Winslow Homer, who later became a famous American artist.

The War Begins

However strongly Lincoln hoped for friendship and peace, he knew that the country was on the verge of war. One of the few federal military posts in the South still occupied by Union troops was Fort Sumter, which sat on an isolated island in the harbor of Charleston, South Carolina. Its commander, Major Robert Anderson, was running out of food. Lincoln agreed to send more supplies. When the Confederates learned this, they sent an order to Major Anderson to surrender. He

Shelled by Confederate guns on the mainland in April 1861, Fort Sumter was severely damaged. Its surviving defenders surrendered a day after the shelling began.

refused, and on April 12, Confederate guns began to batter the fort. Anderson surrendered the next day. The Civil War had begun.

The firing on Fort Sumter rallied most northerners behind their president. Many felt the South needed to be taught a lesson. They were confident that the North, with its superior manpower and industry, could defeat the Confederates in a few weeks. President Lincoln called for 75,000 volunteers to support the small peacetime army. (Many U.S. army officers from the South had resigned and gone home to fight for the Confederacy.)

Lincoln used his executive powers as president to mobilize for war. He issued orders to increase the size of the regular army and navy and ordered a *blockade* of all southern ports along the Atlantic and Gulf coasts. Late in April, volunteers from the North began arriving in Washington to provide protection for the city and to form an army to attack the South in the months to come.

The beginning of the war also rallied the Confederate cause. After Fort Sumter, five more states—Texas, Arkansas, Virginia, North Carolina, and Tennessee—seceded from the Union and brought the Confederate total to eleven states. A Confederate army gathered in Virginia across the Potomac River from Washington, D.C., where the Union army was positioned to defend the capital.

Congress convened in special session on July 4. Lincoln reported his actions and the mostly Republican Congress approved nearly all of them.

The First Major Battle

In July, after months of preparation, the Union army near Washington was ready to attack the Confederate troops across the Potomac River in Virginia. The plan was to drive the Confederate army southward toward Richmond, Virginia, the capital of the Confederate States of America.

Commanded by General Irvin McDowell, Union forces attacked the Confederate army near Manassas, Virginia, on July 21, 1861. (Union soldiers called the spot Bull Run, for a small stream that ran through the battlefield.) The first Union assault went well, driving the Confederates back. Then the Confederates counterattacked, and the inexperienced Union soldiers broke ranks and fled in panic. They crossed the Potomac and straggled up the road toward Washington. Thousands of young men who had never seen battle learned in a few hours how terrible it could be.

The South was overjoyed by its victory, while the North was shocked at its defeat. Many who had expected the war to be short began to realize that it might last a long time. President Lincoln relieved McDowell of command of the army and appointed General George B. McClellan, a model soldier and a superb organizer. McClellan supervised the building of fortifications around Washington and began training his defeated army to become a fighting force. He did his job with great skill and spirit, and he gained the love and support of his men.

However good he was at building and training, McClellan seemed slow to fight. Through the fall of 1861, Lincoln pressed him to attack the Confederate army in Virginia. McClellan explained that he was still preparing. Months passed and nothing seemed to be happening. Finally, in January 1862, an impatient Lincoln issued an executive order requiring the army to move to the attack by February 22. McClellan resented the interference of the president in military matters and stubbornly refused to change his schedule.

General George McClellan helped train and organize the Union army in the East and was a great favorite of the troops.

Fortunately for Lincoln, there was some good war news during the winter. A force led by General Ulysses S. Grant had navigated up the Ohio and Tennessee Rivers into western Tennessee. There, on February 6, Grant captured Fort Henry. He marched his army 12 miles (19 km) overland and attacked Fort Donelson on the Cumberland River. On February 16, the fort surrendered and Grant took its defenders prisoner. These were the first important Union victories.

At Home in the White House

Lincoln spent nearly every waking moment working. He insisted on spending several hours each day meeting with any citizens who lined up at the White House to see him. Outside of these visiting hours, he met with military advisers and his cabinet. He wrote all of his own speeches and much of his correspondence. He had little time for anything else.

Mary Lincoln was thrilled to be first lady. Even before the inauguration, she was picking rugs and fabrics for redecorating the White House, and she spent huge sums on elegant clothes for herself. Sadly, she often had a difficult time in Washington. Wives of eastern politicians refused to attend her social gatherings and made fun of her. Those who did come often found her arrogant.

Willie and Tad enjoyed living in the White House more than their parents. Much to the dismay of the White House staff, the boys were allowed to run anywhere they chose. Tad, who was nine, even wore a Union officer's uniform and made White House guards march around to his orders. Robert, the Lincoln's oldest son, was away studying at Harvard College.

Among Lincoln's few relaxations were carriage rides with Mary around Washington and their evenings at the theater, which he dearly loved. Mary enjoyed planning White House social occasions. In February 1862, she organized an elaborate open house to show off the new White House furnishings and deco-

The Lincoln family in the White House. Robert (standing) was a student at Harvard College for most of the time his father was president. Willie (center) died of a fever in 1862 at the age of 11. Tad (next to his father) was the youngest.

rations. She invited 500 guests, who considered the evening a great success. Sadly, the president and his wife were distracted. Upstairs, their son Willie was ill with a fever, and they each slipped away for a few minutes to sit with him.

Willie probably had typhoid fever, a disease carried in contaminated water. Soon after, his brother Tad also came down with the fever. On February 20, eleven-year-old Willie died. Lincoln was brokenhearted over the boy's death. For weeks afterward he spent time by himself to weep. Mary was even more deeply affected. She did not appear in public for months, and she insisted on wearing black mourning clothes for a year. The couple did not entertain at the White House during the mourning period. Tad fortunately recovered.

War Discouragement

In April 1862, General Grant was involved in another great battle in the West, at Shiloh, Tennessee. He had been surprised by a Confederate attack and nearly lost the battle on the first day. With reinforcements on the second day, he counterattacked and drove the Confederate army from the field. Both armies suffered heavy casualties.

In the East, Lincoln and McClellan continued to disagree. McClellan insisted that attacking near Manassas again would be too risky. Instead, he wanted to ferry his huge army down the Potomac River into Chesapeake Bay. From there, they could attack Richmond from the east. Lincoln pointed out that Washington would be left unguarded. McClellan insisted, however, and Lincoln finally agreed to his plan.

Through the spring, the Union waited expectantly for the battle to begin on the peninsula east of Richmond. The Confederates moved a strong defending army between the Union army and Richmond, but McClellan inched his way closer to Richmond. By the end of May, Union troops could see the church steeples in

Richmond less than 10 miles (16 km) away. Then on May 31, the Confederates attacked, defeating McClellan's armies at Seven Pines and Fair Oaks. Late in June, with further reinforcements, the Confederates attacked again, driving McClellan back to the James River. McClellan's larger, better equipped army had been driven into retreat.

While McClellan refitted his army on the James River, Lincoln put General John Pope in command of the Army of Virginia near Washington. Pope's army crossed into Virginia and prepared to attack Confederate forces at Manassas (Bull Run). Once again the Confederates struck first. They attacked and sent the Union army into a disorganized retreat.

Lincoln was discouraged and depressed. The war was going badly, and he was being pressured by Congress, by his

Fast Facts
THE CIVIL WAR

Who: The United States (the Union or the North) against the Confederate States of America, made up of southern states that had seceded from the Union

When: April 12, 1861–May 1865

Why: Southern states, believing the election of Abraham Lincoln threatened states' rights and slavery, seceded from the United States and fought for their independence. The North fought to restore the southern states to the Union, and later to end slavery.

Where: States along the border between the Union and the Confederacy, especially Virginia and Tennessee. Confederate forces had some early successes, but were overcome by the Union's superior resources. Major northern victories came at Gettysburg, Pennsylvania, and Vicksburg, Mississippi (both July 1863); Atlanta, Georgia (September 1864); and Petersburg and Richmond, Virginia (both April 1865).

Outcome: The Confederate Army of Northern Virginia surrendered to Union forces April 9, 1865, ending the major fighting. The victorious North passed legislation that abolished slavery, gave civil rights to former slaves, and put defeated states under military rule. Efforts to reconstruct the South continued until 1877.

cabinet, and by the newspapers to take action. On September 2, he reluctantly relieved General Pope and recalled General McClellan to take command of the Army of Virginia. The army on the peninsula was ferried by ship back to camps outside Washington.

The Emancipation Proclamation ——————————

President Lincoln was also under pressure from Congress and the people of the North to take action against slavery. He had begun the war to restore the Union, and insisted that the issue of slavery was an incidental issue. By the middle of 1862, however, he began to change his mind. He realized that to break the power of the Confederacy, he had to strike at slavery in the rebellious states. An *Emancipation Proclamation*, freeing the slaves of the Confederacy, would also strengthen his support among opponents of slavery in the North and would discourage Great Britain and other European countries from recognizing or giving help to the South.

Lincoln drafted a document that declared the slaves in the Confederacy "forever free" unless the rebellious states returned to the Union within a specified time. He read his draft to the cabinet. They approved of it, but Secretary of State William Seward urged Lincoln to wait for a Union victory before publishing the proclamation. Lincoln agreed.

Soon after the Confederates won the second Battle of Manassas (Bull Run), General Robert E. Lee set his army on the march to the north and west. They crossed the Potomac River into Union territory in western Maryland. General McClellan and his army were soon moving northward, staying between Lee's army and Washington. On September 17, 1862, the two armies met near the village of Sharpsburg, Maryland, along the banks of Antietam Creek. In the single bloodiest day of the war, the Union army just managed to drive the

An artist's view of a skirmish during the Battle of Antietam (Sharpsburg), where nearly 25,000 men were killed, wounded, or missing in a single day of fighting.

Confederates off the field. Altogether, nearly 25,000 men were reported killed, injured, or missing.

Lincoln saw the battle of Antietam as the victory he had been waiting for. Seven days later, he issued the preliminary Emancipation Proclamation, giving the Confederate states 100 days to join the Union. Otherwise, all slaves in the states named would be freed. Lincoln signed the final proclamation on January 1, 1863, and the slaves of the South were officially freed.

Black Soldiers in the Civil War

Early in the war, Lincoln opposed using African Americans in the Union army, fearing that if he did so, the border states would be angered and switch sides. "To arm the Negroes," Lincoln wrote, "would turn 50,000 bayonets from the loyal Border States against us."

As the North continued to lose battles, however, Lincoln changed his mind. He was urged to use black soldiers by African American Frederick Douglass, himself a former slave. In July 1862, Congress passed an act giving the president the power to recruit African Americans.

Eventually 186,000 black men served in the Union army and about 24,000 in the Union navy. Many black soldiers never saw combat, but were relegated to manual labor and garrison duty. In time, however, some saw action and fought with courage and skill. Some 38,000 black soldiers died. Their dedication to the Union cause was an inspiration to many in the Union, especially to the white soldiers who witnessed their bravery under fire.

☆ ☆ ☆

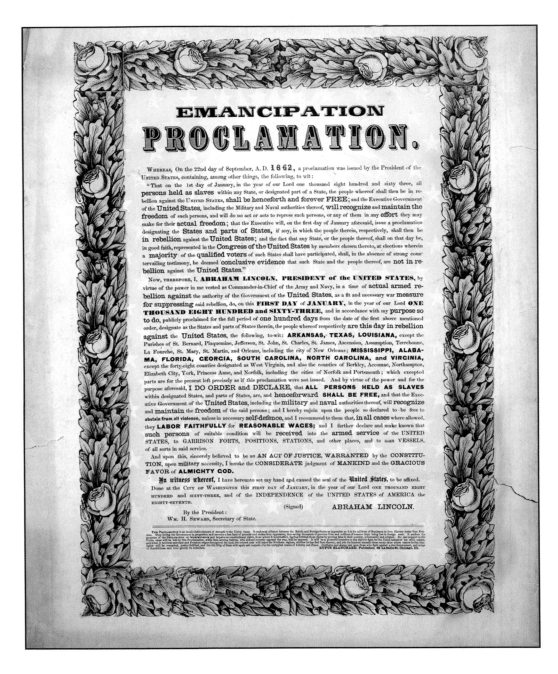

A fancy engraved copy of the Emancipation Proclamation, which announced that slaves in the Confederate states would be freed on January 1, 1863, if the states did not return to the Union.

The Emancipation Proclamation had little immediate effect. The Union government had no power to free slaves in the Confederacy, although some were encouraged to flee north to freedom. The proclamation freed no slaves in Tennessee or in the states remaining in the Union that still allowed slavery, because Lincoln didn't want to lose their support. Even so, the Emancipation Proclamation marked an important change in the war. Northerners who opposed slavery cheered the president's action and renewed their support for Lincoln. Demonstrations in British cities supporting emancipation helped assure that the British government would not give assistance to the South. Once again, Lincoln had affirmed that slavery was not just a political issue but a moral issue as well.

Chapter 5

The Darkest Moment ———————

After the victory at Antietam, Lincoln pleaded with General McClellan to follow the defeated Confederates and inflict further damage on their army. As always, McClellan delayed, claiming that his own army was in need of rest and more supplies.

When six weeks passed, Lincoln revealed his irritation in a letter to the general. "I have just read your dispatch about sore tongued and fatigued horses. Will you pardon me for asking what the horses of your army have done since the battle of Antietam that fatigue anything?" In November 1862, Lincoln removed McClellan from command of the army for the last time.

Once again, Lincoln's desire for action soon backfired. In December, the new general of the Army of the Potomac, Ambrose Burnside, decided to attack the Confederate fortifications at Fredericksburg, Virginia. In one of the worst defeats of the war, line after

After Antietam, Lincoln (in the top hat) visited McClellan (facing Lincoln) and his staff. A few weeks after the photograph was taken, Lincoln removed McClellan from command.

line of Union troops were mowed down by Confederates firing from strong defensive positions. The Union army was forced to retreat once again. In January 1863, after another poorly planned effort to attack the enemy, Burnside resigned, and his command was given to Joseph "Fighting Joe" Hooker.

In April, Hooker marched the army into Virginia to attack the Confederates once again. Union forces seemed poised for a great victory at Chancellorsville when the daring Confederate general, Stonewall Jackson, surprised them by marching around their right flank and attacking at nightfall.

Again, the Union army retreated with heavy losses. (Jackson himself was accidentally shot by one of his own men in the darkness and died of his wounds, a huge loss to the Confederacy.)

Lincoln was despondent. Even the Emancipation Proclamation could not protect him from growing criticism from Congress and from newspapers across the North, which continued to ask when the Union would achieve victory on the battlefield. Lincoln began to wonder if he could survive as president and if the war could ever be won. These were the darkest days of his presidency.

General Robert E. Lee (center) overlooking a battlefield. Lee proved to be a daring and dangerous adversary of the Union armies.

The Turning Point

In June 1863, the Confederate army, commanded by Robert E. Lee, went on the attack once again, invading western Maryland. This time it crossed Maryland into the rich farmlands of south central Pennsylvania. Residents of the region were in a panic.

The Union commander, George Meade, who had replaced Hooker, kept his large and well-supplied army between Lee's army and Washington, then advanced cautiously into Pennsylvania. The two armies met on July 1, 1863, at the edge of Gettysburg, Pennsylvania. The Union army took a strong defensive position in the town and defended it against Confederate attacks. In three days of intense fighting, the Union lost nearly 22,000 men killed, wounded, or missing. The Confederates, who could not afford heavy losses, lost 28,000. Under cover of darkness on the third night, Lee's army began its long retreat to Virginia.

Late on the third day of fighting at Gettysburg, the division commanded by General George Pickett (in the background) charged Union positions (foreground) across a broad, open field. This brave attack failed, and hundreds of attackers were killed or wounded. That night, the Confederates retreated, and the battle was over.

News of the victory reached Washington on the Fourth of July. That same day, General Ulysses S. Grant accepted the surrender of the Confederate force trapped at Vicksburg, Mississippi. Grant and his army had been working for nearly a year to capture this high fortress over the Mississippi River. Soon afterward, the Union army and navy would take possession of the whole Mississippi, cutting the Confederacy in two and allowing shipments of farm goods from the North to reach New Orleans once again.

Finally, the North's huge advantage in wealth and in men had brought two important victories. At the same time, the Confederacy was approaching bankruptcy. It was running out of fighting men and would have increasing difficulty feeding its troops and supplying them with ammunition.

For Lincoln, not all the news was good, however. After the Battle of Gettysburg, the Union generals once again delayed attacking the retreating Confederate forces, allowing them to get safely across the Potomac River into Virginia. Then on July 13, 1863, riots broke out in New York City, protesting the Union's effort to draft new soldiers. About a hundred people were killed (including many African Americans), and Lincoln was forced to send federal troops to help restore order.

Lincoln accepted an invitation to attend the dedication of the military cemetery at Gettysburg in November 1863. The thousands who had been killed there had been buried on a part of the battlefield, and the dedication was a major event. The featured speaker of the day was Edward Everett of Massachusetts, who spoke for about two hours to a large crowd. Finally, near the end of the ceremony, President Lincoln stood to give his brief remarks.

The speech was so short that many in the crowd were not paying full attention. Yet in the following days, it was printed in newspapers throughout the Union. Over the years, it has become the most memorable and familiar speech in the country's history. In it, Lincoln summarized the meaning of the war and his

At Gettysburg four months after the battle, Lincoln delivered his Gettysburg Address to a huge crowd, gathered to dedicate part of the field as a cemetery for the thousands who had died in battle.

The Gettysburg Address

Four score and seven years ago, our fathers brought forth on this continent, a new nation, conceived in Liberty, and dedicated to the proposition that all men are created equal.

Now we are engaged in a great civil war, testing whether that nation or any other nation so conceived and so dedicated, can long endure. We are met on a great battle-field of that war. We have come to dedicate a portion of that field as a final resting place for those who here gave their lives that the nation might live. It is altogether fitting and proper that we should do this.

But, in a larger sense, we can not dedicate—we can not consecrate—we can not hallow—this ground. The brave men, living and dead, who struggled here, have consecrated it, far above our poor power to add or detract. The world will little note, nor long remember what we say here, but it can never forget what they did here. It is for us the living, rather, to be dedicated here to the unfinished work which they who fought here have thus far so nobly advanced. It is rather for us to be here dedicated to the great task remaining before us— that from these honored dead we take increased devotion to that cause for which they gave the last full measure of devotion—that we here highly resolve that these dead shall not have died in vain—that this nation, under God, shall have a new birth of freedom—and that government of the people, by the people, for the people, shall not perish from the earth.

☆ ☆ ☆

hope that it would bring "a new birth of freedom" to the country. He ended by urging the nation to rededicate itself to the task of winning the war.

Edward Everett later wrote the president, "I should be glad, if . . . I came as near the central idea of the occasion in two hours as you did in two minutes."

New Commanders

By early 1864, Lincoln was frustrated with his eastern generals, who seemed unable to pin down Lee's armies in Virginia. In March, he appointed General Ulysses Grant General-in-Chief of the Union Armies. Grant would plan strategy for all the fighting forces and would personally take charge of the Army of Northern Virginia. The Union armies now at Chattanooga would be directed by General William Tecumseh Sherman.

General Ulysses S. Grant helped plan and carry out the strategy that finally defeated the Confederacy.

Grant planned a general *offensive* to begin early in May. Sherman was to push Confederate forces out of Chattanooga and into northern Georgia with the aim of capturing Atlanta. Grant would engage the Confederate forces of Robert E. Lee in Virginia with the aim of capturing Richmond, the capital of the Confederacy.

Grant first attacked the Confederates in the region known as the Wilderness, near Chancellorsville. In a grim two-day battle, he was unable to force

Lee's forces to retreat and his army suffered huge casualties—17,000 killed, wounded, or missing. Unlike earlier Union generals in the east, Grant did not retreat after a difficult battle. Instead, he moved his army sideways to the east and south, toward Richmond, forcing Lee's army to move to meet him. The armies fought again at Spotsylvania with similar results. The Union army suffered 17,000 more casualties. This pattern continued through May and into June.

General Sherman was also fighting a series of costly battles, driving the Confederate defenders through the mountains and hills of Georgia, closer and closer to Atlanta. The Confederates fought bravely and gave up ground slowly. Here, too, Union losses were heavy.

Northern newspapers reported the battles of Grant and Sherman as great victories, but as readers learned more about the huge casualties, they were not so sure. Long lists of local men killed, wounded, and missing appeared regularly in newspapers throughout the Union. Earlier generals had reported heavy losses, but not day after day and week after week. Even Abraham Lincoln was sickened by the terrific loss of life. Washington served as a hospital center for the wounded from Grant's army, and Lincoln could often see the long lines of horse-drawn ambulances arriving from the battle-fields.

Election Fever

Lincoln had a campaign of his own to direct. He was up for reelection in November. To run, first, he had to win the Republican nomination. Many in the party considered him a poor candidate. Radical Republicans believed he was not committed enough to a total victory over the Confederacy. Conservative Republicans believed he was too harsh. They were weary of war and wanted the president to end the war by diplomacy and negotiation.

Lincoln refused to compromise with either group. Instead, he worked behind the scenes, lining up support for his nomination. His opponents never found a promising candidate to run against the president. At the Republican convention in June, he was easily nominated. The convention dropped Lincoln's current vice president, Hannibal Hamlin, and nominated instead Andrew Johnson, a loyal Democrat from Tennessee, to attract votes from the border states.

Late in August, the Democratic convention met. It wrote a "peace" *platform* (a statement of principles), demanding negotiations with the Confederacy to end the war. But the candidate they nominated, former general George B. McClellan, said that he would not be bound by the peace plank in the party platform.

The election was decided partly by news from the battlefields. In June, General Grant had slipped around Richmond and surrounded the town of Petersburg, south of the capital. There he endangered Richmond's supply lines

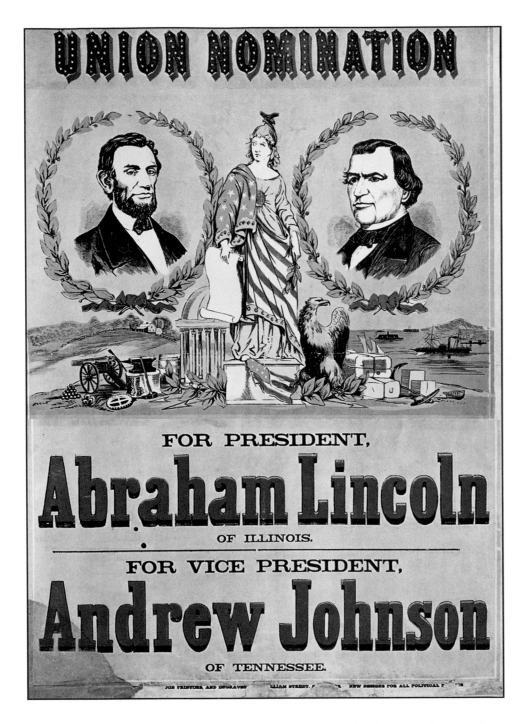

A campaign poster for Abraham Lincoln and Andrew Johnson for the 1864 presidential campaign. They ran on the Union ticket, hoping to attract the votes of northern Democrats as well as Republicans.

from the south. Grant's dangerous position tied down most of Lee's army near Richmond. General Sherman's army surrounded Atlanta, cutting off its supplies of food and ammunition. On September 2, the city surrendered and was burned.

These victories made a powerful case for Lincoln's reelection. His popularity soared, and he carried all but three states in the Union. Even so, Democratic candidate McClellan gained 45 percent of the popular vote.

The Union army's capture of Atlanta, the most important city in Georgia, was a serious blow to the Confederacy. Much of the city was destroyed by fire during the evacuation.

Sherman's March

After securing Atlanta, General Sherman made a daring move. In November, without any sure way to supply his army, he set out to the east through Georgia toward Savannah on the Atlantic coast. Because his men had no other way to feed themselves, they commandeered grain and farm animals to feed the troops. They also looted homes and terrorized the residents in a swath 20 miles (32 km) wide from Atlanta to the sea. The Confederates had no available force to oppose him. Sherman captured Savannah on Christmas Eve, and he presented it to Lincoln by telegraph as a Christmas gift.

Sherman's march through Georgia became a notorious example of an army's cruelty to civilians. Yet today most historians believe Sherman's "cruelty" saved lives in both the North and the South by ending the war more quickly.

Preparing for Peace

Through the winter, President Lincoln embarked on a new campaign. When Congress convened in December, he urged them to pass the 13th Amendment to the Constitution, officially *abolishing* slavery in the United States. After long and sometimes heated debate, both the House and the Senate passed the amendment by the needed two-thirds majority on January 31, 1865. The amendment went

The States During the Presidency of Abraham Lincoln

NEVADA
(1864)

WEST
VIRGINIA
(1863)

STATES WHEN PRESIDENT TOOK OFFICE

JOINED UNION DURING PRESIDENCY (YEAR JOINED IN PARENTHESES)

into effect only after it was *ratified* (or approved) by three-fourths of the states in December 1865, yet the North rejoiced. The amendment went far beyond the Emancipation Proclamation, ending slavery in the United States and all its territories.

On March 4, 1865, after being sworn in for a second term, Lincoln delivered one of the shortest inaugural addresses ever. He wondered what the intention of the Almighty may have been in a war that had now lasted nearly four years. He observed that both sides "read the same Bible, and pray to the same God, and each invokes His aid against the other." He suggested that the war was a punishment on both sides for the "offense" of slavery. This seemed an odd and uncomfortable thought only weeks before a Union victory. Yet Lincoln concluded his address with these comforting words:

> With malice toward none; with charity for all; with firmness in the
> right, as God gives us to see the right, let us strive on to finish the work
> we are in; to bind up the nation's wounds; to care for him who shall
> have borne the battle, and for his widow, and his orphan—to do all
> which may achieve and cherish a just, and a lasting peace, among
> ourselves, and with all nations.

War's End

On April 3, General Grant overran the town of Petersburg, and within hours, the Confederate government began fleeing Richmond. Federal troops soon occupied the Confederate capital.

Lincoln was eager to visit Richmond himself. His advisers were horrified that he would take such a risk, but Lincoln was determined. He arrived in Richmond with no ceremony, accompanied by his eleven-year-old son Tad and a small military guard. The white residents of Richmond stayed indoors, but African American slaves rushed out to greet him. They knew that they would soon be free. Lincoln visited the deserted home of Confederate president Jefferson Davis, had lunch with the new military governor, and rode through parts of the city. He also met privately with representatives of the Confederacy.

In the next few days, General Grant's army was pursuing General Lee's tattered forces south of Richmond. Finally Lee offered his army's surrender in a letter to Grant. The two generals met on April 9, in the small settlement called Appomattox Court House. On Lincoln's orders, Grant's terms of surrender were generous. The Confederate forces were allowed to go home in time to plant seed for the year's crops. In the following weeks, other smaller Confederate armies surrendered. The long, bloody Civil War came to an end.

An artist's conception of the meeting at Appomattox in April 1865. General Robert E. Lee (right) surrendered his army to General Grant (left) in the parlor of a private home.

Death at Ford's Theatre

On April 14, Abraham and Mary Lincoln decided to go to the theater. They invited General Grant and his wife, who were visiting Washington, but they declined. Instead, the president invited a young army officer and his fiancée. At one point during the play, Lincoln held his wife's hand. She chided him, asking what their guests would think if they saw. "They won't think anything of it," he replied.

A few moments later, an intruder quietly entered the Lincolns' unguarded box and fired a bullet at close range into the back of the president's head.

John Wilkes Booth shot President Lincoln in the presidential box (top center), then jumped down to the stage and would escape out a back door. In this artist's version, he has a knife in his hand and is shouting something to the crowd.

John Wilkes Booth

Several people in Ford's Theatre that night recognized the assassin as John Wilkes Booth. He was part of a distinguished family of actors and a successful actor himself. He had not fought for the Confederacy, but he had deep sympathy for the South. He blamed Lincoln for the war and for the South's suffering.

Booth had broken his ankle in his leap to the stage, but he managed to reach the stage door, where a horse was waiting to carry him to safety. The assassination of Lincoln was part of a larger plot to kill several leaders in the Union government. Another would-be assassin broke into the house of Secretary of State Seward, who was in bed recovering from a serious carriage accident, but failed to kill him. Others assassins failed to attack their targets.

Booth and an accomplice, David Herold, escaped to Virginia. Twelve days later, federal troops cornered him in a tobacco barn. When he refused to surrender, he was shot to death. Herold and seven other conspirators were later tried and convicted. Four were hanged.

☆ ☆ ☆

The theater broke into pandemonium. The *assassin* leaped to the stage and escaped. The unconscious Lincoln was carried from the theater to a rooming house across the street, where he died the next morning.

The nation was stunned by the president's death. His death at the very moment the war ended was impossible to understand. After a solemn funeral service in the capital, his body was borne on a funeral railroad car from

Washington to Springfield, Illinois. On the 1,700-mile (2,700-km) journey the car stopped at many cities, where the body lay in state to be viewed by thousands of mourners. The train reached Springfield on May 3, and Abraham Lincoln was buried there.

Chapter 6

Aftermath

Lincoln's death set the country on a difficult and often painful journey. His new vice president, Andrew Johnson, was sworn in as president hours after Lincoln died. Johnson, a loyal Democrat from Tennessee, was not prepared to deal with the huge problems of restoring the states of the Confederacy. Radical Republicans in Congress distrusted him and were determined to pass their extreme plans for reconstructing the Confederate states. Many felt that the South deserved punishment for secession and the war.

Gradually Congress restricted President Johnson's executive powers because he would not work with them or agree to any compromise. When he defied their restrictions, Congress impeached him, hoping to convict him of "crimes" and remove him from office. At his impeachment trial, the Senate was the jury. A majority of senators voted to convict, but they fell one vote short of the two-thirds majority needed to remove him. Disgraced, Johnson served the rest of his term quietly.

The Lincoln Family

The Lincoln family also faced difficult times. Mary Lincoln was so distraught over her husband's death that she was unable to attend his funeral. She tried to find some consolation in travel, spending long periods in Europe. In 1871, her youngest son, Tad, died of tuberculosis, causing another long period of mourning and regret. In 1875, she became so disturbed that her son Robert committed her to a mental hospital for a brief time. She died in Springfield in 1882.

Robert Lincoln, who was nearly 22 when his father died, became a successful lawyer in Chicago and served as secretary of war to Presidents James Garfield and Chester Arthur. In 1881, he was with Garfield when an assassin shot and fatally wounded the president in the Washington train station. Twenty years later, Lincoln was at the American Exposition in Buffalo, New York, on the day an assassin shot and fatally wounded President William McKinley. After being so near three presidential assassinations, Lincoln resolved that he would never again appear in public with a president. He became a prominent and successful business executive and died in 1926 at age 83.

Mary Todd Lincoln dressed in mourning after the death of her son Willie in 1862. After her husband's death in 1865, she suffered the death of her youngest son, Tad, in 1871.

Who Was Abraham Lincoln?

As the years passed, Americans remained fascinated by Abraham Lincoln. The solemn Lincoln Memorial was built in Washington, D.C., to commemorate his life and achievements. His striking face was stamped on billions of U.S. coins and was carved into the face of Mount Rushmore with the images of George Washington, Thomas Jefferson, and Theodore Roosevelt.

Hundreds of books appeared, some for scholars and many for general readers, exploring his life and trying to understand the qualities that set him apart from other presidents and national heroes. Some portrayed him as a saint who had freed the slaves and sacrificed his life for his country. Some concentrated on his humble beginnings and his rise as a shrewd prairie lawyer. Still others described the dark sides of his character—his deep depressions and his powerful political ambition.

Lincoln was a complicated man. Yet in his speeches and writing, he was able to express his hopes and aspirations in simple language. He helped keep the Union together through four of its darkest years, and gave meaning and importance to the sacrifice of the men who fought and died in its armies. As the war came to a close, he was eager to restore the people of the Confederacy to the United States, and urged the victorious Union to show charity and forgiveness.

The Lincoln Memorial in Washington, D.C. At its center is a larger-than-life marble statue of the president.

Behind the scenes, Lincoln was also a master politician. His enemies in the North criticized him for being indecisive and slow to act. Often he had a clearer sense of purpose and timing than his critics. Using charm, flattery, and sometimes threats, he got people with widely differing views to work together toward common goals. He was able to work even with leaders who despised him to accomplish the nation's objectives.

Lincoln was faced with more difficult decisions than any previous president. When he entered office, the Union was breaking apart. With a war approaching, the North had no great army, few weapons, and no military strategy. Its leaders were divided, and its goals were unclear. Lincoln had to be more than a politician. As the war began, he had to balance political, military, economic, and moral claims. The human costs of the war horrified him, yet he gradually learned to be a great war president. When the people of the country were war-weary and it seemed they might give up, he found the words to inspire, encourage, and comfort them.

He was accused of taking dictatorial powers, holding suspected traitors without trial, and enforcing stern military discipline. Yet he saw the war as a battle to protect the values that helped to establish the United States—especially the belief that all men are entitled to human rights, including "life, liberty, and the pursuit of happiness."

Many of the presidents before Lincoln's election seemed to be crushed and defeated by the pressures of the office. By contrast, Lincoln seemed to grow in the office from year to year. As the war progressed and the suffering increased, he found some inner strength that allowed him to lead, encourage, and comfort. As the war came to an end, he persuaded Congress to abolish slavery, then urged generous terms to reunite the country.

What would he have done to "bind up the nation's wounds" in the remaining years of his term? No one will ever know. In the end, the anger and hatreds stirred up by the great Civil War ended his life too soon.

Fast Facts   Abraham Lincoln

Birth:	February 12, 1809
Birthplace:	Sinking Springs Farm near Hogdenville, Kentucky
Parents:	Thomas Lincoln (died 1851) and Nancy Hanks Lincoln (died 1818)
	Stepmother, Sarah Bush Johnston Lincoln, married Thomas Lincoln 1819 (died 1869)
Brothers & Sisters:	Sarah (1807–1828)
	Thomas (born 1812, died in infancy)
Education:	About one year of formal schooling in Kentucky and Indiana
Occupation:	Lawyer, legislator
Marriage:	To Mary Ann Todd, November 4, 1842
Children:	(*See* First Lady Fast Facts at right)
Political Parties:	Whig, Republican
Public Offices:	1834–1842 Representative, Illinois General Assembly
	1847–1849 Member, U.S. House of Representatives
	1861–1865 Sixteenth President of the United States
His Vice Presidents:	Hannibal Hamlin (1861–1865)
	Andrew Johnson (1865)
Major Actions as President:	1861 Apr. Declared a state of war against Confederacy
	1863 Jan. Issued Emancipation Proclamation
	1863 Nov. Delivered Gettysburg Address
	1864 Mar. Appointed Ulysses S. Grant General-in-Chief of Union Armies
	1864 Nov. Elected to second term as president
	1864 Dec. Recommended 13th Amendment to Congress
	1865 Mar. Inaugurated to second term
	1865 Apr. Visited Richmond, captured Confederate capital; Confederate Army of Northern Virginia surrendered
	1865 Apr. Assassinated by John Wilkes Booth
Firsts:	First president to be assassinated.
	Only president to hold a U.S. patent, for a device that lifts ships over shoals using air chambers
	First president to grow a beard
Death:	April 15, 1865, in Washington, D.C.
Age at Death:	56 years
Burial Place:	Oak Ridge Cemetery, Springfield, Illinois

Fast Facts Mary Todd Lincoln

Birth:	December 13, 1818
Birthplace:	Lexington, Kentucky
Parents:	Robert Smith Todd and Eliza Parker Todd (died 1825)
	Stepmother, Elizabeth Humphries Todd, married Robert Todd 1826
Brothers & Sisters:	Elizabeth (1813–1888)
	Frances Jane (1815–1899)
	Levi Oldham (1817–1864)
	Robert Parker (1820–1822)
	Ann Marie (1824–1881)
	George Rogers (1825–1902)
	(Eight half brothers and sisters born between 1827 and 1841)
Education:	Shelby Female Academy and Madame Mentelle's boarding school for girls in Lexington, Kentucky
Children:	Robert Todd (1843–1926)
	Edward "Eddie" Baker (1846–1850)
	William "Willie" Wallace (1850–1862)
	Thomas "Tad" (1853–1871)
Death:	July 16, 1882
Age at Death:	63 years
Burial Place:	Oak Ridge Cemetery, Springfield, Illinois

Timeline

1809	1816	1818	1828	1830
Abraham Lincoln born, February 12.	The family moves to Indiana.	His mother, Nancy Hanks Lincoln, dies. His father remarries the next year.	Lincoln pilots a flatboat to New Orleans.	The Lincolns move to Illinois.

1836	1837	1842	1843	1844
Receives his license to practice law.	Moves to Springfield, Illinois.	Marries Mary Ann Todd, November 4.	First son, Robert, is born.	The Lincolns buy a house in Springfield.

1858	1859	1860	1861	1862
Debates Stephen Douglas in campaign for the U.S. Senate, August–October.	Loses election for Senate to Douglas, January.	Nominated for president by the Republicans; elected November 6.	Inaugurated as 16th president, March 4; the Civil War begins, April 12.	Eleven-year-old son Willie dies, February 20; Union forces win the Battle of Antietam, September 17.

1831
Lincoln leaves his family and settles in New Salem, Illinois.

1832
Serves in the militia during the Black Hawk War.

1833
Tries his hand as postmaster, surveyor, and store owner.

1834
Elected to the Illinois General Assembly, serves until 1842.

1835
First love Ann Rutledge dies.

1846
Son, Edward "Eddie," born. Lincoln elected to the U.S. House of Representatives, serves 1847–1849.

1850
Eddie dies; son William "Willie" born in December.

1853
Son Thomas "Tad" born.

1854
Lincoln runs for U.S. Senate and is defeated.

1856
Joins the new Republican party.

1863
Lincoln issues Emancipation Proclamation, January 1; Union armies win the Battle of Gettysburg, July 1–3; Lincoln delivers Gettysburg Address, November 19.

1864
Appoints Ulysses S. Grant General-in-Chief of Union forces, March; Grant begins overland campaign against Confederates in Virginia, May.

1864
Union army under General Sherman captures Atlanta, September 2; Lincoln elected to second term, November 8.

1865
Confederate general Robert E. Lee surrenders his army to Ulysses S. Grant, April 9.

1865
Lincoln is shot in Ford's Theatre by John Wilkes Booth April 14 and dies the following morning.

Glossary

abolish: to end; the 13th Amendment abolished slavery in the United States

arsenal: a government installation where weapons and ammunition are stored

assassin: a person who kills a public official or leader

blockade: an action by naval ships to close enemy ports by keeping ships from entering or leaving

electoral college: in the U.S. government, the body that meets to officially elect a president and vice president, based on the popular vote in each state

Emancipation Proclamation: the official announcement freeing the slaves of Confederate states issued by President Lincoln on January 1, 1863

Fugitive Slave Act: a law passed as part of the Compromise of 1850 committing the federal government to help track down runaway slaves in the North and return them to their masters in the South

offensive: a plan of attack on an enemy army or armies

platform: a document approved by a political party as a statement of its goals

popular sovereignty: in the 1850s, the view that residents of a new state should decide by a vote whether to allow or prohibit slavery

ratify: to approve; a Constitutional amendment goes into effect when three-fourths of the states have ratified it

secede: to withdraw from a government; the southern states seceded from the United States in 1860 and 1861

unanimous: describes a vote in which all voters agree

Further Reading

★ ★ ★ ★ ★

Anthony, Carl Sferrazza. *America's First Families: An Inside View of 200 Years of Private Life in the White House.* New York: Touchstone, 2000.

Blassingame, Wyatt. *The Look-It-Up Book of Presidents.* Revised edition. New York: Random House, 1996.

Diller, Daniel C., and Stephen L. Robertson. *The Presidents, First Ladies, and Vice Presidents: White House Biographies, 1789–2001.* Washington, DC: CQ Press, 2001.

Holzer, Harold, editor. *Abraham Lincoln, The Writer: A Treasury of His Greatest Speeches and Letters.* Honesdale, PA: Boyds Mill Press, 2000.

Otfinoski, Steven. *John Wilkes Booth and the Civil War.* Woodbridge, CT: Blackbirch Press, 1999.

Paletta, Lu Ann, and Fred Worth. *The World Almanac of Presidential Facts.* New York: World Almanac, 1988.

Shorto, Russell. *Abraham Lincoln and the End of Slavery.* Brookfield, CT: Millbrook Press, 1991.

Whitney, David C., and Robin Vaughn Whitney. *The American Presidents.* 8th edition. Pleasantville, NY: Reader's Digest, 1993.

MORE ADVANCED READING

Donald, David. *Lincoln.* New York: Simon & Schuster, 1995.

Guelzo, Allen C. *Abraham Lincoln: Redeemer President.* Grand Rapids, MI: William B. Eerdmans Publishing Co., 1999.

Lincoln, Abraham. *Abraham Lincoln: Speeches and Writings 1832–1858.* Edited by Don E. Fehrenbacher. New York: Library of America, 1989.

Lincoln, Abraham. *Abraham Lincoln: Speeches and Writings 1859–1865.* Edited by Don E. Fehrenbacher. New York: Library of America, 1989.

McPherson, James M. *Battle Cry of Freedom: The Civil War Era.* New York: Oxford University Press, 1988.

Oates, Stephen B. *With Malice Toward None: The Life of Abraham Lincoln.* New York: Harper & Row, 1977.

Places to Visit

★ ★ ★ ★ ★

Lincoln Birthplace National Historic Site
2995 Lincoln Farm Road
Hodgenville, KY 42748
(270) 358-3137 or 3138

The birthplace of Lincoln includes what is possibly the log cabin he was born in and a visitors' center. A reproduction of his second home, on Knob Creek Farm, is ten miles away.

Lincoln Boyhood National Memorial
P.O. Box 1816
Lincoln City, IN 47552
(812) 937-4541

This 200-acre site includes the farm where Lincoln lived from 1816 to 1830 and the burial site of his mother, Nancy Hanks Lincoln.

Lincoln's New Salem State Historic Site
2 miles south of Petersburg, Illinois, on SR 97
Petersburg, IL 62675
(217) 632-4000

A reconstruction of the town, no longer in existence, where Lincoln lived from 1831 to 1837.

Lincoln Home Visitors Center and National Historic Site
426 South Seventh Street
Springfield, IL 62701
(217) 492-4241

The home Lincoln and his family lived in from 1844 until he became president in 1861. The home is the centerpiece of a four-block restored historic neighborhood.

Lincoln's Tomb State Historic Site
Oak Ridge Cemetery
Springfield, IL 62702
(217) 782-2717

Lincoln is buried here along with Mary Lincoln and three of their four children.

The White House
1600 Pennsylvania Avenue NW
Washington, DC 20500
Visitors' Office (202) 456-7041

The Lincoln family lived here a little more than four years.

Ford's Theatre National Historical Site
900 Ohio Drive SW
Washington, DC 20024
(202) 426-6924

The place where Lincoln was assassinated on April 14, 1865. It is still a working theater and houses a museum dealing with the assassination.

Lincoln Memorial
23rd Street NW
Washington, DC
(202) 426-6841

One of the greatest memorials to any president, it is located in Potomac Park and was dedicated in 1922.

Online Sites of Interest

★ **The American Presidency**

http://gi.grolier.com/presidents/ea/bios/16plinc.html

A detailed and informative biography of Lincoln, including a useful bibliography.

★ **Internet Public Library, Presidents of the United States (IPL POTUS)**

http://www.ipl.org/div/potus/alincoln/html

Includes concise information about Lincoln and his presidency and a number of links to other sites including biographies and other Internet resources. The site is managed by the School of Information at the University of Michigan.

★ **AmericanPresident.org**

http://www.americanpresident.org/history/abrahamlincoln/

Provides useful information on Lincoln's early life, his presidency, and the times in which he lived. The site is managed by the Miller Center for Public Affairs at the University of Virginia.

★ **Abraham Lincoln Online**

http://showcase.netins.net/web/creative/lincoln.html

Contains news about Lincoln sites and events, guided tours, and much more.

★ **Presidential Inaugural Addresses**

http://www.bartleby.com/124/pres31.html

Lincoln's complete first and second inaugural addresses are here as well as access to the inaugural address of every other president.

★ **The White House**

http://www.whitehouse.gov

Information about the current president and vice president, White House history and tours; biographies of past presidents and their families, a virtual tour of the historic building, current events, trivia quizzes, and much more.

Table of Presidents

1. George Washington

2. John Adams

3. Thomas Jefferson

4. James Madison

	1. George Washington	2. John Adams	3. Thomas Jefferson	4. James Madison
Took office	Apr 30 1789	Mar 4 1797	Mar 4 1801	Mar 4 1809
Left office	Mar 3 1797	Mar 3 1801	Mar 3 1809	Mar 3 1817
Birthplace	Westmoreland Co, VA	Braintree, MA	Shadwell, VA	Port Conway, VA
Birth date	Feb 22 1732	Oct 20 1735	Apr 13 1743	Mar 16 1751
Death date	Dec 14 1799	July 4 1826	July 4 1826	June 28 1836

9. William H. Harrison

10. John Tyler

11. James K. Polk

12. Zachary Taylor

	9. William H. Harrison	10. John Tyler	11. James K. Polk	12. Zachary Taylor
Took office	Mar 4 1841	Apr 6 1841	Mar 4 1845	Mar 5 1849
Left office	**Apr 4 1841•**	Mar 3 1845	Mar 3 1849	**July 9 1850•**
Birthplace	Berkeley, VA	Greenway, VA	Mecklenburg Co, NC	Barboursville, VA
Birth date	Feb 9 1773	Mar 29 1790	Nov 2 1795	Nov 24 1784
Death date	Apr 4 1841	Jan 18 1862	June 15 1849	July 9 1850

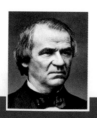

17. Andrew Johnson

18. Ulysses S. Grant

19. Rutherford B. Hayes

20. James A. Garfield

	17. Andrew Johnson	18. Ulysses S. Grant	19. Rutherford B. Hayes	20. James A. Garfield
Took office	Apr 15 1865	Mar 4 1869	Mar 5 1877	Mar 4 1881
Left office	Mar 3 1869	Mar 3 1877	Mar 3 1881	**Sept 19 1881•**
Birthplace	Raleigh, NC	Point Pleasant, OH	Delaware, OH	Orange, OH
Birth date	Dec 29 1808	Apr 27 1822	Oct 4 1822	Nov 19 1831
Death date	July 31 1875	July 23 1885	Jan 17 1893	Sept 19 1881

5. James Monroe

Mar 4 1817

Mar 3 1825

Westmoreland Co, VA

Apr 28 1758

July 4 1831

6. John Quincy Adams

Mar 4 1825

Mar 3 1829

Braintree, MA

July 11 1767

Feb 23 1848

7. Andrew Jackson

Mar 4 1829

Mar 3 1837

The Waxhaws, SC

Mar 15 1767

June 8 1845

8. Martin Van Buren

Mar 4 1837

Mar 3 1841

Kinderhook, NY

Dec 5 1782

July 24 1862

13. Millard Fillmore

July 9 1850

Mar 3 1853

Locke Township, NY

Jan 7 1800

Mar 8 1874

14. Franklin Pierce

Mar 4 1853

Mar 3 1857

Hillsborough, NH

Nov 23 1804

Oct 8 1869

15. James Buchanan

Mar 4 1857

Mar 3 1861

Cove Gap, PA

Apr 23 1791

June 1 1868

16. Abraham Lincoln

Mar 4 1861

Apr 15 1865•

Hardin Co, KY

Feb 12 1809

Apr 15 1865

21. Chester A. Arthur

Sept 19 1881

Mar 3 1885

Fairfield, VT

Oct 5 1830

Nov 18 1886

22. Grover Cleveland

Mar 4 1885

Mar 3 1889

Caldwell, NJ

Mar 18 1837

June 24 1908

23. Benjamin Harrison

Mar 4 1889

Mar 3 1893

North Bend, OH

Aug 20 1833

Mar 13 1901

24. Grover Cleveland

Mar 4 1893

Mar 3 1897

Caldwell, NJ

Mar 18 1837

June 24 1908

	25. William McKinley	**26. Theodore Roosevelt**	**27. William H. Taft**	**28. Woodrow Wilson**
Took office	Mar 4 1897	Sept 14 1901	Mar 4 1909	Mar 4 1913
Left office	**Sept 14 1901•**	Mar 3 1909	Mar 3 1913	Mar 3 1921
Birthplace	Niles, OH	New York, NY	Cincinnati, OH	Staunton, VA
Birth date	Jan 29 1843	Oct 27 1858	Sept 15 1857	Dec 28 1856
Death date	Sept 14 1901	Jan 6 1919	Mar 8 1930	Feb 3 1924

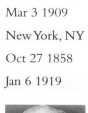

	33. Harry S. Truman	**34. Dwight D. Eisenhower**	**35. John F. Kennedy**	**36. Lyndon B. Johnson**
Took office	Apr 12 1945	Jan 20 1953	Jan 20 1961	Nov 22 1963
Left office	Jan 20 1953	Jan 20 1961	**Nov 22 1963•**	Jan 20 1969
Birthplace	Lamar, MO	Denison, TX	Brookline, MA	Johnson City, TX
Birth date	May 8 1884	Oct 14 1890	May 29 1917	Aug 27 1908
Death date	Dec 26 1972	Mar 28 1969	Nov 22 1963	Jan 22 1973

	41. George Bush	**42. Bill Clinton**	**43. George W. Bush**	
Took office	Jan 20 1989	Jan 20 1993	Jan 20 2001	
Left office	Jan 20 1993	Jan 20 2001	—	
Birthplace	Milton, MA	Hope, AR	New Haven, CT	
Birth date	June 12 1924	Aug 19 1946	July 6 1946	
Death date	—	—		

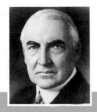

29. Warren G. Harding	**30. Calvin Coolidge**	**31. Herbert Hoover**	**32. Franklin D. Roosevelt**
Mar 4 1921	Aug 2 1923	Mar 4 1929	Mar 4 1933
Aug 2 1923•	Mar 3 1929	Mar 3 1933	**Apr 12 1945•**
Blooming Grove, OH	Plymouth, VT	West Branch, IA	Hyde Park, NY
Nov 21 1865	July 4 1872	Aug 10 1874	Jan 30 1882
Aug 2 1923	Jan 5 1933	Oct 20 1964	Apr 12 1945

37. Richard M. Nixon	**38. Gerald R. Ford**	**39. Jimmy Carter**	**40. Ronald Reagan**
Jan 20 1969	Aug 9 1974	Jan 20 1977	Jan 20 1981
Aug 9 1974★	Jan 20 1977	Jan 20 1981	Jan 20 1989
Yorba Linda, CA	Omaha, NE	Plains, GA	Tampico, IL
Jan 9 1913	July 14 1913	Oct 1 1924	Feb 11 1911
Apr 22 1994	—	—	—

• Indicates the president died while in office.

★ Richard Nixon resigned before his term expired.

Index

About the Author

Steven Otfinoski attended Boston University and graduated from Antioch College in Yellow Springs, Ohio. He has written more than a hundred books for young adults and children. He is the author of *William Henry Harrison* and *Rutherford B. Hayes* in the Encyclopedia of Presidents series. Among his recent books are *African Americans in the Visual Arts; African Americans in the Performing Arts; Bugsy Siegel and the Postwar Boom; John Wilkes Booth and the Civil War; Marco Polo: To China and Back; Francisco Coronado: In Search of the Seven Cities of Gold; Nations in Transition: Afghanistan; It's My State! Maryland; It's My State! Washington;* and *Celebrate the States: Georgia.* He has also written two books on popular music for adults: *The Golden Age of Rock Instrumentals* and *The Golden Age of Novelty Songs.*

Mr. Otfinoski lives in Connecticut with his wife Beverly, a teacher and editor, and their two children, Daniel and Martha. Among his hobbies are reading, traveling, listening to and collecting popular music of the 1950s and 1960s, and playing tennis.